DESERT
SURVIVOR'S
GUIDE

DESERT SURVIVOR'S GUIDE

Rory Storm

Illustrated by Mei Lim

Scholastic Inc.

New York   Toronto   London   Auckland   Sydney
Mexico City   New Delhi   Hong Kong   Buenos Aires

ISBN 0-439-32855-1

Text copyright © 2001 by Rory Storm.
Illustrations © 2001 by Mei Lim.

All rights reserved. Published by Scholastic Inc.
SCHOLASTIC and associated logos are trademarks and/or registered trademarks of Scholastic Inc.

12 11 10 9 8 7 6 5 4 3 2 1   1 2 3 4 5 6/0

Printed in the U.S.A.   40
First Scholastic printing, October 2001

CONTENTS

WARNING!

This guide is to learn about extreme survival situations. The techniques are not suitable for use at home and are only to be used in real emergencies.

Rory

SO YOU WANNA BE A DESERT SURVIVOR?

CHAPTER ONE

SO YOU WANNA BE A DESERT SURVIVOR?

What on earth gave you the idea that you could take on the desert? You've got to be a real tough cookie to make it in these arid areas of the world, you know. I've been in and out of survival situations all my life and, I don't mind confessing, deserts scare the heck out of me. Not because I can't survive in a desert environment, but because I know just what damage the desert can inflict on the fainthearted, the unwary, or the ill-prepared.

I guess you'd probably call my feelings for the desert a love/hate relationship. The desert is mesmerisingly stark and beautiful, yet it can be the most unforgiving place on earth. Survival here is tough beyond belief.

Nevertheless, there will always be those crazy enough to take on the desert challenge. Each year, adventurers turn up for the most grueling motor race in the world — the Paris-Dakar rally, even though they know that contestants are frequently killed during the 6,213-mile (10,000-km) race that crosses the Sahara desert to end in Dakar, Senegal.

But something about the desert draws the flamboyant and eccentric spirit. Take, for instance, English parish priest, Geoffrey Howard, who crossed the Sahara on foot with only the clothes on his back and his belongings in a wheelbarrow. Not the type you might find in your backyard, mind you, but a Chinese sailing wheelbarrow, no less! Ninety-four days and almost two thousand miles later he achieved his goal, having raised a good deal for charity and with a new world record under his belt. How wacky and wonderful is that!

BE PREPARED

On a more serious note, if you are going to be a desert survivor you're obviously going to need some good, basic survival skills, which you'll find plenty of later in the book. Yet, you'll need more than just skill. Do you have any idea what other qualities you might need? Well, for starters, you'll need to be resourceful, resilient, and extremely determined.

You'll also have to be decisive. Of all the survival environments, the desert is the most demanding in terms of requiring speedy decisions and quick reactions. You don't have the luxury of pondering the best course of action. Without water, you will last at best five days in the desert — and that's resting in the shade! If you try to walk out, you'll last one day.

FINDING YOUR WAY

Conditions in the desert can also change very rapidly due to violent sandstorms and, believe it or not, torrential downpours, so you must be adaptable, too. Plus, you'll need good navigational skills since you've got to find your way in a featureless natural world or, possibly more confusing still, in a place where the features change due to sandstorms!

Whether you navigate by the stars or compass, a good sense of direction is essential. In animals, this sense appears to be instinctive and has often been used to good effect to escape danger, as was the case with Sandy, a mongrel who was the mascot of the Royal Signals company based in Alexandria, Egypt, during the Second World War. As the Germans pushed the British army back, Sandy, together with his company, was evacuated to El Alamein.

Unfortunately, the Germans captured the truck in which Sandy was traveling. The soldiers were taken prisoner and Sandy was thrown out.

Remarkably, a few weeks later, Sandy reappeared in Alexandria, having walked across 140 miles (225 km) of desert, surviving the heat of the sun and the cold desert nights amidst fierce fighting. Not only that, but he managed to navigate the labyrinthine backstreets of Alexandria to find his barracks where he was greeted with a hero's welcome.

WHAT TO EXPECT

In *Desert Survivor's Guide*, we look at ways to provide yourself with the lifesaving essentials of water and shelter from the heat and glare of the desert sun. You'll also need to avoid the many dangers that lurk in the desert, so we'll explore ways of dealing with anything from snake attacks to quicksand.

Once you've absorbed this essential survival know-how, you'll have a chance to read about how some brave individuals put the theory to the test and withstood the perils of the desert. From those who find themselves in the desert by misadventure to those brave few who set out on military missions behind enemy lines, I'm sure you'll be fascinated and inspired by their tales of courage and determination.

Once you've gotten that far, you should have enough desert savvy to come up with some blinding solutions to the "What if . . . ?" chapter and to sail through the Desert Survivor's Brain-teaser challenge, where you're invited to compile your very own survival plan to save you and your companions.

LADY LUCK

Those who live in the harsh outback environment will tell you that there is one more commodity that is needed to help you survive against the desert. That elusive quality is luck.

Like the time when a young man found himself lost in the desert. Dehydrated, he stumbled around looking for water and, in his delirium, he stripped off all his clothes. As if all this weren't bad enough, the poor unfortunate chap then fell headlong into a clump of spiny cacti. As he thrashed around, trying to get out, his body was covered in deep cuts and long scratches — cactus spines are nasty. He eventually scrambled out but, remarkably, he did not bleed. By rights, he should have been dripping blood everywhere, which would have seriously compromised his chances of survival. However, because your blood thickens when you're dehydrated, he didn't spill a drop. His luck held, and he was picked up by a search party. The funny thing is, once they gave him some fluids, his copious lacerations started to bleed profusely. Luckily for him, he was now in the company of medical experts who could deal with his many injuries. What an amazing and lucky escape!

Let's hope that luck will smile on you, too, if you ever find yourself in a Desert Survival Situation.

So, without further ado, let's knuckle down and see how we can survive in the desert. Bring it on!

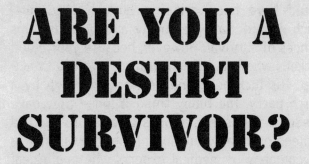

ARE YOU A DESERT SURVIVOR?

ARE YOU A DESERT SURVIVOR?

Of all the environments in which to survive, the desert is probably the hardest. So, if you think you know something about desert survival, I will be mighty impressed.

Here's your chance to show off — a pretty tough quiz on desert survival. Think you're up to it? Well, let's see how you do.

Oh, and don't be worried if you're finding it a bit difficult. There are lots of opportunities later in the book to bone up on some great survival tips and desert knowledge, plus the lowdown on some real-life survivors and their hair-raising desert adventures.

1. The world's largest desert is:
A The Arabian
B The Sahara
C The Gobi
D The Atacama

2. Your friend is bitten on the calf by a rattlesnake. Do you:
A apply a tourniquet above the bite
B suck out the poison
C put his leg in hot water
D wrap an elastic bandage from the knee to the ankle

3. Mesas and buttes are types of:
A cacti
B Arabian sandwiches
C desert robes
D columns of rocks and hills

4. The lowest point of dry land in the world is found in:
A Death Valley, U.S.A.
B The Great Desert, Australia
C The Andes, Peru
D The South Pole

5. After sending a distress signal with your location, your plane crash-lands in the desert. Should you:
A get as far away from it as possible
B try to retrace your flight path
C stay near the wreckage, using it for shelter
D try to repair the engines for takeoff again

6. Sometimes desert travelers see what they think is a pool of water in the distance. When they reach the spot, they find only dry sand. This effect is called a:
A mirage
B miracle
C meringue
D mirza

7. The frilled lizard of the Australian desert runs on its back legs. It does this so:
A it can see predators approaching
B it can meet and chat with other frilled lizards
C it can reach its food in the low branches of trees
D it minimizes its contact with the hot sand

8. Cacti can live for up to:
A 10 years
B 50 years
C 100 years
D 200 years

9. If you were caught unprepared by a pamperos, would you:
A try to take shelter from the wind
B try to climb up it
C ask him to let you go
D fight to the death

10. You would make a solar still in the desert to get:
A whisky
B a photo image
C water
D a hot meal

11. If you were caught in a sudden sandstorm, would you:
A cover yourself thoroughly and take shelter behind your gear
B keep walking
C stop and have a picnic
D turn and face into the direction of the wind

12. People who have no permanent home but travel from place to place building temporary shelters are known as:
A Tribesmen
B Nomads
C Sheikhs
D Herdsmen

ANSWERS

So how did you do? Did you breeze through it, or was the going tougher than you expected? Give yourself one point for every correct answer — I trust you to play fair — and we'll see just how desert savvy you are at the end.

1.b The world's largest desert is the Sahara, with an area of 5,600,000 square kilometers. Temperatures can vary between 126°F (52.2°C) at midday to 26°F (-3.3°C) at night.

2.d This kind of bandaging prevents the toxin from spreading rapidly and being taken up by the lymphatic system. Despite what you see in old Westerns, you should never apply a tourniquet or try to cut or suck out the poison. Placing the wound in cool water is helpful, but hot water would simply spread the poison faster.

3.d Buttes are columns of rock that have been worn away by the elements and mesas are large, flat-topped hills that have been formed through the effects of wind, water, and heat wearing away the rock. I must admit, though, they do sound a little like an exotic packed lunch.

4.a At 282 feet (86 m) below sea level, Death Valley is the lowest point of dry land in the world. Air temperatures reach 135°F (57°C), and ground temperatures 79°C. Wise up, the Andes of Peru are some of the highest mountains in the world. But if you thought the South Pole was an obvious red herring, you might be surprised to learn that both the North and South Poles are considered cold "deserts."

5.c It is much easier for rescuers to spot wreckage in the vastness of the desert than it is to find a survivor wandering around alone. If no one knew of your dilemma and you decided to walk out, you'd go the shortest route to safety — and that's probably not your flight path. Even if you're a brilliant mechanic and manage to repair the engines, it's unlikely that you'd get a decent runway to take off — assuming you were brave enough or crazy enough to try it!

6.a A mirage must be one of the most soul-destroying experiences for a desert survivor. Could you keep going after having your hopes raised and dashed by a mirage?

7.d The sand is blisteringly hot and most animals who live in the desert have developed ways to reduce their contact with this hot surface. If you chose "c," tell me how many leafy trees have you seen in the desert? And if you chose "b," you're obviously nuts.

8.d Remarkable though it may seem, a cactus can live up to 200 years.

9.a Being caught by the pamperos sounds very nasty, doesn't it? In fact, pamperos is the name given to the strong, drying winds that blow much of the time in the Patagonian desert of South America.

10.c We'll find out how to make a solar still later in the book because water is your primary need in the desert. You certainly don't need whisky or photographs — although it would be good if you could just rustle up a hot meal in this way.

11.a Particles of sand traveling at up to hurricane-force wind speeds get absolutely everywhere and being sandblasted is very painful, so you need to get yourself covered up, especially your ears, eyes, nose, and mouth. In fact, you can even die if you're exposed to a sandstorm for too long. So I don't recommend any of the other options, unless you like sand in your sandwiches of course!

12.b Nomads are on the move all the time. You're right in thinking that tribesmen, sheikhs, and herdsmen all live in the desert, but they tend to live in permanent homes and villages.

SCORING

Tally up your points and then check out your desert survival rating. Hopefully, you're up there with the best of them but if not, don't despair, there's plenty of time to become an ace desert rat before the end of the book.

> **0-4 points:**
> Better luck next time. I think you'd agree that you've got a bit of work to do before it's safe to let you loose in the desert.

> **5-8 points:**
> Not bad at all. With a bit of extra effort you'll be guiding us all to safety.

> **9-12 points:**
> Amazing. You must be some kind of genius. You've earned the title of King Rat. Well done. But, when you've finished taking a bow, it's time to get down to some hard work and find out a bit more about surviving in the desert.

So let's get started, shall we?

BASIC
DESERT
SURVIVAL
SKILLS

BASIC DESERT SURVIVAL SKILLS

Deserts are not the kind of places where you just go for a casual walk. They are seriously dangerous and, although they vary in their nature from rocky plateaus to sand dunes, all are inhospitable and difficult to survive in. Stunningly beautiful, I'll concede, but deadly.

So, from this, I have to conclude that if you find yourself in a survival situation in the desert, it's probably because you've run into disaster while crossing the desert either by aircraft or by vehicle.

Knowing how extreme and perilous the desert environment can be, I'm sure you'd have the sense to pack a survival kit before venturing into or over the desert. In this chapter, we'll touch on some of the equipment and skills you'll need at your disposal if you ever find yourself stranded in the desert.

Remember, deserts are usually unpeopled because there isn't enough water or vegetation to sustain permanent communities. So, without help readily at hand, it really is up to you — your skill, your tenacity and determination, your resourcefulness — to get you and your fellow survivors through this ordeal and back to safety.

DRESSED FOR THE OCCASION

You need clothing that will protect your body from the heat of the sun during the day and from the extreme cold of the desert night. Your whole body has to be covered as protection against both the sun and the discomfort of sandstorms, which are plentiful.

The loose robes of traditional Arab dress have evolved to suit the desert climate and environment ideally, so let's take a leaf out of their book, shall we . . .

- **Clothing should be loose and lightweight. A long-sleeved shirt and full-length pants are ideal.**

- **A hat is essential to protect the head from the sun. Choose one with a broad brim and/or a neck flap. If you can't lay your hands on one of those, then improvise — use a bandanna, towel, or spare shirt to protect your neck and head.**

- **Always carry plenty of sunscreen when traveling in the desert and use it profusely.**

- **The eyes need to be protected from the glare of the sun and the fine sand at all costs. Wear tinted UV protection sunglasses or goggles.**

• Good footwear is essential in the desert because the scorching sand during the day and intense cold at night can cause blistering and cracking of the soles of your feet. Ideally you should have thick-soled boots. Make sure you remove sand, stones, or insects from your boots regularly as they can cause blisters and wounds. Keep sand and stones out by improvising some "puttees" — bind cloth, bandage, or any material over the top of your boots and up over your pant legs and lower leg. A neat and ingenious solution!

• Carry warm clothing or bedding for use at night.

Desert Survivor's Tip

If you don't have protection for your eyes, improvise some goggles by cutting pinholes or slits in a strip of film from your camera and attach it with string. Also, darken the skin under your eyes with charcoal from your fire as this will cut down on the reflected glare.

Desert Survivor's Tip

Always check your boots before putting
them on in the morning — they make a
warm and cozy bed for scorpions and snakes!
You've been warned.

PLAN OF ACTION

If you find yourself stranded in the desert,
whether it's due to a downed aircraft or crashed
or broken-down vehicle, you have to make an
immediate plan of action. You have to weigh the
pros and cons of staying put or walking out. Take
the following criteria into consideration when
coming to a decision:

- What are your chances of rescue? Who
  knows your route and itinerary?

- Can you contact the outside world by
  radio or mobile phone?

- Can you establish your location?

- Is any of your party injured and unable
  to walk?

- What sort of resources do you have
  available to you and how long will they last?

- How much water do you have available and how much can each person carry?

- How far is it to safety and how long will it take you to get there?

- Are you in good enough physical shape to make a grueling desert march? (Here you have to be brutally honest with yourself.)

Desert Survivor's Tip

Commercial airplanes that are forced to crash-land in the desert usually do so quite successfully. For an emergency landing, make sure you follow the captain's instructions fully and get out of the plane as soon as possible after landing, in case of fire. Once you've got the "all clear," depending upon what information has been radioed to the authorities, passengers should stay with the aircraft. The chances of rescue are high since search aircraft are usually less than 24 hours away and planes are supplied with plenty of water and provisions.

In general, if you have a good supply of water with the aircraft or vehicle, and good reason to believe that you'll be rescued, i.e. you sent a Mayday message with your location and know it was received or you were on your planned route, then you should stay with the wreckage. If not, you have little choice but to try to walk out.

GETTING WATER

In the desert, your first priority is water. You need a minimum of 7 to 8 pints (4 to 5 litres) of water a day to even think about walking out safely and, since water in the desert is in short supply (obviously, I hear you say), then you must conserve it the best way you can. In desert temperatures of 122°F (50°C), without any water, you'll last, at best, five days, and that's without exerting any energy. This time is halved if you walk, even at night!

So, it's imperative to locate and collect water.

RAIN

Contrary to popular belief, rain does fall in the desert. It tends to arrive in violent and brief thunderstorms causing flash floods (see page 48). This rainwater soon disappears and you shouldn't sit around waiting for rainfall, which is, let's face it, a bit hit and miss, but pockets may remain where natural rock cisterns protect it from the sun.

DEW

The wide temperature differences between day and night in the desert mean that condensation will form on any metal sheeting such as the hood of a car or wing of an airplane.

In the early morning, this dew can be mopped up using an item of clean clothing, which can then be wrung out into a container. You should be able to collect a pint an hour if you get the technique right.

PLANTS

Many desert plants store drinkable water. Look for cacti, which have no root system and store water in their bodies. It's not easy to get the sap out because of the protective spines, but if you manage it, the pulp can be squeezed to produce an emergency water supply. One word of warning though: the tall, multi-fingered saguaro cactus that is found mainly in Arizona is extremely poisonous, so avoid it like the plague.

Palms are a gift in the desert because they supply an excellent source of drinkable fluid and sometimes, in the case of the coconut palm, food.

Trees can also give you an idea of how deep below the surface groundwater can be found because of their varying root systems. For example, water can be expected about 3.3 feet (1 m) below the surface by a palm tree but nearly 13 feet (4 m) by a willow or cottonwood tree.

Desert Survivor's Tip
Finding Water
Look for:

- The movement or tracks of birds, animals, and insects. These usually lead to water.

- Valleys, gullies, and watercourses where water normally collects at the lowest point, on the outside of a bend.

- Clouds, rain, and lightning — head that way.

- Any kind of greenery, especially palm trees.

- Rocky outcrops — water may collect in hollows in the rocks.

- Caves — look for trickles of water that may suggest a larger supply. Probe for these and try to suck out the water.

- Distinctive signs such as piles of animal droppings or human-made rock constructions that may indicate a water hole.

- Signs of the passage of humans or camels will always lead to water.

Fact File

A Bushman of the Kalahari gets water by finding the deepest part of a dried-up watercourse, then digging a hole in the sand until he finds moist sand (about an arm's length usually). He then takes a long tube (about 5 feet; 1.5 m), made from the stem of a bush with a soft core, and winds dry grass around one end. He inserts the tube into the hole and packs the sand around it, stamping it down with his feet. He sucks hard on the tube for a couple of minutes and then, what d'ya know, water comes out.

COLLECTING WATER

A solar still condenses the moisture in the atmosphere and can work very effectively in just about any environment. Not only does it collect water but it also purifies it so it can be used with brackish water and even seawater.

It's simple to make and is a really useful tool.

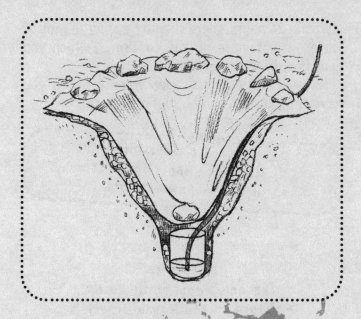

- Dig a hole in the ground about 3 feet (1 m) across and 2.5 feet (75 cm) deep at the center.

- Put a wide container in the middle and place one end of a drinking tube, if available, into the container.

- Place a plastic sheet loosely over the hole, weighting it down around the edges with rocks or sand to make it airtight. The sheet should droop down into the hole and the drinking tube should stick out.

- Find a fist-sized stone and carefully place it at the center of the sheet, directly above the container. Make sure the sheeting doesn't touch the sides of the hole or the earth will absorb your precious condensed water.

Within 24 hours, there should be about a pint of water, if not more, in the container, which you can then drink through the tube.

One still will only just keep you alive so if you have the materials to build more, do so.

P.S. If it rains, your solar still will also catch the rainwater — a double whammy! Cool.

Fact File
The only regular supply of moisture to the Namib desert is the fog that rolls in from the South Atlantic Ocean each morning. A local beetle has developed a unique way of making the most of this unusual water source — it stands with its back to the incoming fog and allows moisture to condense on its body. It then catches the water droplets as they trickle down its back into its mouth! Pretty smart for a beetle, huh!

CHAPTER THREE

DESERT SHELTER

Apart from the need to find water, there is one other prerequisite in the desert and that is the need for shelter. The human body needs shelter from the fierce sun during the day and protection from the biting cold at night.

Since it is likely that you are in your current predicament due to transport failure — either a plane crash or a vehicle breakdown — then you have some ready-made shelter at hand.

On the other hand, if your transport was destroyed by fire or if you are alone in the desert for some other reason, then you are going to have to rely on your resourcefulness to make some shelter for yourself. Don't despair — even in the barren landscape of the world's deserts, there is always something the ingenious and determined can do to help themselves.

Fact File
The deserts of the United States are crisscrossed with roads. Once you find a track, you should be able to make contact pretty soon with a passing vehicle.

TYPES OF SHELTER

Make full use of your natural surroundings when looking for shelter and remember to work in the cool of the early morning or evening.

AIRCRAFT OR VEHICLE SHELTER

If you've got the use of unserviceable transport, there's little sense in making work for yourself by building something else.

During the heat of the day, shelter in the shade under the wings of an aircraft (it's too hot inside). If you drape a parachute or sheeting over the wing, this will protect you still further against sand, flies, and the sun.

At night, crawl inside the body of the plane (fuselage), which should retain some of the heat of the day. If possible, close the doors for warmth and protection against sandstorms.

If the plane is not safe or cannot be sealed, then the life rafts will give you protection against sandstorms, but you must secure them down well.

A vehicle will get too hot to shelter inside during the day, unless it has a convertible roof, but it can provide protection at night. Use any available sheeting to provide shade during the day and to keep you warm in the vehicle at night.

Fact File
The camp tent of the desert nomads is designed to let the breeze under its lower edges so that air can circulate.

STONE SHELTER

Find a rocky outcrop and stretch your canvas, poncho, or other material from the top of the outcrop to the ground, weighting down each end with stones, sand, etc.

Rocks are plentiful in most deserts. Pile them into a semicircular windbreak and stretch a groundsheet down to the ground, weighted on the top and bottom, to provide shelter.

With a little more effort, a stone shelter, or sangar as it's known in the forces, can be transformed into a circular stone "house," with piled walls and a groundsheet, survival blanket, or poncho overhead to give shade. At night, use it as a blanket. Such a construction has done me proud on many an occasion, I can tell you.

Desert Survivor's Tip
Remember that snakes and scorpions also look for warmth at night and your cozy shelter may be the warmest thing around!

Fact File
Sangar comes from the Persian
word for stone.

SAND SHELTER

As a lifesaver, you can simply scoop out a shallow hollow in the sand and cover it with a groundsheet or any other sheeting to make a primitive emergency shelter from the rays of the sun. This is known as a "scrape."

Draping a sheet over scrubby bushes or rocks is another alternative.

Use the side of an existing dune or build a mound of sand. Then anchor your material with weights or plenty of sand on top of the sandbank and stretch the material down to the ground and anchor it there.

Desert Survivor's Tip

In any kind of shelter, two layers of material separated are better than one. A gap of about 16 inches (40 cm) between them allows the air to circulate and drastically reduces the temperature. Keep the lightest-colored material on the outside to reflect the sun's rays.

Fact File

Only one-third of the world's deserts are sand-covered. However, sand dunes can be up to 1000 feet (300 m) high and 15 miles (24 km) long and these massive dunes, called ergs, are actually moving — remarkably about 30 cm a day.

Desert Survivor's Tip

If you have no material help, look for shade or shelter at natural desert features such as rock cairns, caves, or overhangs. Look for features that will provide the most shade. Virtually any natural shelter can be improved by building a small rock wall in front to protect against wind and sandstorms.

BUILDING A DOUBLE SHEET SHELTER

1 Scoop a depression out of the ground.

2 Find four large rocks and place at the corners of a groundsheet stretched out over the "scrape."

3 Place smaller rocks on top to anchor the groundsheet.

4 Place a second groundsheet on top, leaving several inches in between, if possible.

This can also be secured with sand or rocks or, if available, it can be tethered with improvised guy ropes.

MAKING A FIRE

Once you've got yourself some shelter and a supply of water, you can think about a fire to protect you from the nighttime cold, for cooking, if you're lucky enough to have food, and for signaling — which may save your life.

In some deserts, fires have to be kept small because of the lack of anything to burn. However, in desert regions covered with dry scrub, a fire should be relatively easy to make, although it is not a very efficient fuel and scrub fires don't tend to last very long.

If you are traveling at night, try to gather any natural kindling and fuel you encounter as you go and keep it with you.

Signal fires are normally only feasible if you stay with your vehicle or aircraft and use tires or oil to make a highly visible plume of black smoke. If these are in limited supply, make sure a rescue plane stands a chance of spotting your signal fire before you light it.

Desert Survivor's Tip

There is a plant that grows in the Nevada desert that is called the kerosene plant. This burns exceptionally well and produces a good, hot fire.

Fact File

During World War II, the British soldiers in North Africa, who were known as "Desert Rats," improvised a simple yet efficient cooker. They used liquid fuel from their vehicles and poured it into a can that they'd previously half filled with sand. After a few minutes of letting it soak in, they put tinder on the top and lit it. This would burn for about five minutes and was hot enough to boil water or fry an egg. This became known as a "Benghazi" stove.

Warning: Although a Benghazi stove is safe, you should never play with or set fire to an inflammable liquid or volatile fuel. Never add extra fuel while the stove (or any fire for that matter) is lighted and don't touch the can, which becomes extremely hot. Always let an adult handle matches, fuel, and/or fire.

DESERT
SURVIVAL
STORIES

DESERT SURVIVAL STORIES

Now you know in theory what you're supposed to do in an emergency, so let's see what a handful of brave individuals did in reality when they found themselves in dire straits in the desert.

NEW YEAR'S EVE DISASTER

New Year's Eve 1998 was Robert Martin's last night in Oman and he decided to celebrate it quietly camping in the desert with a friend, Regina. Robert was German and he had been working in Oman for an international oil company, but luckily for him, he also knew some basic desert survival skills.

As he and his friend returned home, their vehicle got bogged down in soft sand. Unperturbed, Robert used his air jack to get the car out of danger but, unbeknownst to him, the jack had been wrongly positioned and it had broken the fuel pump. After a few miles, the car stopped. Robert couldn't get it started again so, because it was getting late in the afternoon, they decided to camp out for another night.

STAYING CALM, STAYING PUT

The next morning, the car still wouldn't start and Robert and Regina had to decide whether to stay put or to walk to the nearest village. Robert's survival training helped sway the decision and so the couple stayed put. They had wisely left details of their route with friends back in the city so they calculated that a search party would find them in three days or so. They worked out how much water and supplies they had left and started to ration it out.

Nobody passed by. They waited. They even made up card games to pass the time. As the days passed, they became increasingly tempted to walk out, but, despite the urge to do something positive, the couple stuck to their original plan and stayed put.

Desert Survivor's Tip

Unless you're able to produce lots of black smoke, daytime signal fires are a waste of time in the desert. If you're still with your transportation, you can burn tires, seats, and oil, to produce black smoke. However, at night, if you can collect enough scrub bushes, a nighttime signal fire can be prepared.

SEARCH PLANES

On the fourth day, they heard the first helicopter but, frustratingly, they were not spotted. In fact, during their ordeal, they saw several rescue planes but their signal fires were not spotted because the smoke was too thin.

Finally, on the eighth day, they lit the tires from the car and they were picked up. Robert was amazed because when they took off and looked down from the rescue plane, even from only 656 feet (200 m) up, they couldn't see the car anymore.

It really was like searching for a needle in a haystack. Robert and Regina did everything right and still they were lucky to be found — could you have resisted the temptation to walk toward the village after more than a week waiting? It's a hard call, isn't it.

Desert Survivor's Tip

Low-flying search aircraft can often be heard but not seen because of the heat haze. In this case, flash your heliograph or mirror toward the sound of the aircraft, using a small circular action. The flash is very conspicuous and I know that this simple action has saved lives in the past.

The new heliographs have been designed to reflect the sun's rays accurately so you can target a rescue aircraft over a distance of up to 12.5 miles (20 km). If you don't have a heliograph, a mirror will do.

OUTSTANDING COURAGE

When the Gulf War of 1991 was over, the people of Kuwait were left with a deadly legacy. The retreating Iraqi forces had mined large areas of their country.

An off-duty British Air Force officer was driving his car along a beach road one day when he heard the screams of a young boy. He pulled over and realized that two kids who'd been playing football had stepped on and triggered a mine. One boy was lying silently in the sand while the other was crying out in pain.

SELFLESS ACT

Although he had no training in mine clearance, the officer could not stand by and do nothing. He entered the minefield on his stomach, using an unorthodox breaststroke swimming action to gently push the sand (and any mines) away from him as he progressed toward the injured boys.

He finally reached the motionless body of one of the boys and gently dragged him back down the track that he'd cleared to safety.

After one miraculous escape, now he had to steel himself to reenter the minefield to rescue the second boy. Could you have gone back in, do you think?

Fact File
There are over 60 million mines laid worldwide. Although laid during conflicts, most mines are triggered by innocent civilians. Around 30 people per day — two-thirds of whom are children — accidentally trigger land mines and, in the vast majority of cases, this results in amputation of a limb at best, if not death. Most de-miners are local people who have been sent on a short training course. A new motion-powered detector (a pendulum inside generates power) is being pioneered and it is hoped that this simple technology will help in the ongoing battle against land mines.

ALLAH WILLING

The officer slowly inched his way toward the second casualty who was, by this time, hysterical and still screaming in agony. To his amazement, a Kuwaiti doctor, who had also been passing in his car, walked along the track he had so painstakingly made, stepped over the prostrate officer, and boldly walked to the injured boy. He injected him with a strong sedative and then retraced his steps, leaving the British officer to retrieve the sedated casualty.

The second boy was successfully brought clear of the minefield to safety and they were both whisked off to the hospital for treatment. By then, the unknown Kuwaiti doctor had driven off and, somewhat shaken, the British officer carried on with his journey. He was later awarded a medal for bravery for this act of selflessness and courage.

I'd say both he and the unknown doctor were true heroes, wouldn't you agree?

TRAIN RIDE TO TROUBLE

Back in the late 1990s, two young guys decided to hitch a lift on the Southern Pacific, known as the "Gray Ghost" freight train to Salt Lake City. At lunchtime, they crept into the train yard and hid on the top of an empty car carrier.

They waited all afternoon and then, suddenly, the engine belched out black clouds of diesel smoke and the 3-mile (4.8 km-)-long train lurched forward. The train picked up speed and soon the pair were congratulating themselves on hitching a free ride to Salt Lake City.

DISASTER AROUND THE NEXT BEND

The pair continued to enjoy the late afternoon sun on the roof of the auto-carrier car when suddenly something black flashed over the head of one guy. It was a low-hanging power line and the other man, who was taller at over six feet, was not so lucky. The line caught him in the head and picked him up. Fortunately, he was able to free himself and he fell, shaken, onto the steel floor of the car. If the line had been an inch or two lower, it would have caught his neck and he would have been decapitated. A very narrow escape, wouldn't you say, but the drama wasn't over yet!

ABANDONED IN THE DESERT

Later that day, the train came to a little town called Alturas, in California. Here the train stopped briefly and the pair, still shaken from their earlier near disaster, took the opportunity to get inside one of the car carriers.

In the middle of the night, the train slowed again in a place called Carlen, Nevada, for a change of crew. Remarkably, the train didn't stop but just slowed so that the new crew could jump aboard and the old crew could jump off. The train just kept rumbling on through the darkness into the desert night.

Some time later, the crew started to run some checks on the train. It kept stopping and starting and, in their sleepy state, the hitchhikers were glad when it stopped for good. What they didn't realize was that their car carrier, along with several others, had been sidetracked out in the middle of the desert, somewhere on the border between Utah and Nevada, and the train had gone on without them.

CHAPTER FOUR

This was a fairly desperate situation. For all they knew, the train could be left there indefinitely. It was 150 miles (241 km) across the Nevada badlands to Salt Lake City and they had very little water. The desert seemed to be devoid of vegetation — no cactus, no sagebrush, just dry alkali salt flats as far as the eye could see. When they looked back down the track, they could see a solitary tree on the horizon. Just how hopeless do you think they must have felt at this point?

GOOD FORTUNE

The pair set off walking along the track in the burning desert sun. For the next hundred miles or so ahead of them, there was no sign of civilization. The chances of survival were remote.

Remarkably, after they had walked about ten miles and were feeling completely despondent, tired, and thirsty, they saw a truck carrying a train work crew who were out to mend some track. They frantically flagged the truck down and discovered that it was another 100 miles to Salt Lake City — they would certainly have perished if the truck had not come along.

The crew told them that there was a small town about twenty miles back down the track. So, refreshed and replenished with valuable water, the two set off. They retraced their steps back through the desert past the train, and eventually came to the tree that they had seen on the horizon from the train car. Fortunately for the hapless pair, there was a solitary house by the tree. An old man lived alone there and he allowed them to use his water hose.

Refreshed, they set off again to complete the last ten miles or so to Montello, the town the train crew had mentioned. As they neared the small town, a road joined the train track and, exhausted, they crossed over, collapsed on their packs, and stuck out their thumbs.

After some time, an old hay truck passed by and the farmer picked up the disheveled pair and took them into town. The boys were in luck, yet again. They had hit Montello on the most important day of the year for the small local population — it was the annual Montello Watermelon Festival and the guys gorged themselves on free watermelon.

I never learned whether they ever made it to Salt Lake City or not but I think this very close shave might have cured their temptation to jump train cars, don't you.

Desert Survivor's Tip
Don't Try This at Home

Jumping trains is extremely dangerous and those who attempt it are often killed or maimed. You should never, under any circumstances, attempt this. Moreover, it is illegal and dishonest and not to be condoned.

AUSSIE ADVENTURE

In 1984, two dispatch riders from London were coming to the end of their around-the-world bike ride. Bob and John were crossing the Simpson Desert in Australia on their way to Alice Springs.

Unfortunately, after thousands of miles of safe riding, Bob somersaulted his bike on the desert road and was knocked unconscious in the fall. John pitched the tent by the side of the road and managed to get Bob into it. John then waited by the side of the road in the sweltering heat for help to arrive.

Many hours later, a car pulled up. The driver left what he could spare — a half bottle of water and a raw chicken — and promised to send help when he got home. However, the distances in Australia are vast and home was about 400 miles (643 km) farther up the road.

ROAST DINNER

Things were looking bleak for Bob and John. They were stranded hundreds of miles from habitation in the middle of an unforgiving desert. Nonetheless, John managed to light a fire and started to cook the chicken. Bob eventually regained consciousness to the smell of roasting chicken! A surreal moment, I'm sure.

The next day, as no help had arrived and their provisions were exhausted, the guys decided to try to save themselves. They managed to make some repairs to Bob's bike and to straighten out the bent parts. Remarkably, the bike worked and the lucky pair limped off once again for Alice Springs.

They eventually sold their bikes in Sydney and, with the proceeds, bought an airline ticket back to London.

A lucky escape, wouldn't you say.

Fact File
Flash Floods
One of the most frightening features of desert life is a flash flood. The water from a sudden storm rushes along the parched gully or a dry riverbed, known in parts of Africa and Asia as a wadi. So much water hits the ground during a desert storm that it cannot soak away. It builds into a wall of water 3.28 feet (1 m) or more high, surging along faster than a person can run. Everything in the flood's path is dragged along with it, including boulders and any poor desert animals or people who fail to reach high ground in time. So always be wary of traveling along the floor of steep-sided gullies that are difficult to leave in a hurry.

GREAT
DESERT
EXPLORERS

GREAT DESERT EXPLORERS

It takes a certain type of person to have enough courage and curiosity to set off into unknown and uncharted territory. Of course, nowadays, there's precious little of our globe that hasn't been explored and yet still those with a sense of adventure and an inquisitive nature can find exciting challenges.

It was years ago that the great age of exploration took place. We owe a great debt to the men and women who charted our globe, and none are more deserving of our gratitude than those who explored and survived in the desert lands.

TREKKING ACROSS AUSTRALIA

Although Australia was colonized in the late 1700s, most settlements were on the coastline of Australia. Over the course of 30 or so years, a number of expeditions set out to explore and map the desert interior.

In 1859, the South Australian government offered money to the first person to cross the continent from south to north. Would you have been tempted by the prize money? Well, two separate expeditions set out to claim the reward.

CHAPTER FIVE

BRAVE ADVENTURERS

Robert O'Hara Burke and his companion, William Wills, imported camels from India to help them to cross Australia. Unfortunately, the camels didn't fare too well down under, and most were eventually eaten by the explorers.

Burke and Wills set out from Melbourne and reached the Gulf of Carpentaria on the north coast. However, the expedition was disorganized and neither man knew how to survive well in the harsh desert environment. Of the four men in the final party, only one survived. Despite their undoubted achievement, both Burke and Wills died on the return journey. John King, the survivor, was found living with the Aborigines. It was only their knowledge of desert conditions that allowed him to survive.

THIRD TIME LUCKY

John Stuart, on the other hand, was an experienced explorer who knew how to survive in the outback. He set out from Adelaide and tried to cross the center of the continent. However, he was turned back in the Northern Territory by Aborigines who set fire to the bush to stop Stuart from advancing into their land.

He set out a second time, but the long stretches of thorny bush in the desert scrublands defeated him and he had to turn back.

Finally, in 1862, Stuart managed to cross the desert interior of Australia and his epic journey opened up the whole of the continent for settlement and farming. Do you think you'd be determined enough to try three times, or would you have taken the Aborigines' hint the first time?

Desert Survivor's Tip

Native Australians, commonly known as Aborigines, arrived on the continent over 40,000 years ago. They have perfected survival skills in the punishing interior deserts and survival experts look to them to enhance their expertise of desert survival techniques.

Aboriginal peoples are hunter-gatherers. They catch kangaroos and other animals by throwing a boomerang at them. It returns to the thrower if it doesn't hit the target. They also collect wild plants, nuts, and berries to eat. A great Aborigine delicacy is the witchetty grub. It's a big, fat, white maggotlike bug that they dig out from the roots of trees and then eat alive. Could you bring yourself to eat one? A good source of protein, but not very appetizing, I fear.

Fact File

In 1803, the French sold the west side of North America — later known as the Louisiana Purchase — to the United States. President Thomas Jefferson wanted to find out more about his new acquisition so he sent his personal secretary, Meriwether Lewis, and William Clark, a former army officer, to explore it. It took them two years to follow the Missouri river from St. Louis over the Rockies, down the Columbia River to the Pacific coast. On their return trip via the Yellowstone River to St. Louis, they were joined by Sacajawea, a member of the Sheshone tribe who spoke many native languages and acted as an interpreter for the explorers.

Fact File

Ibn Battuta, a Muslim traveler in the 1300s, devoted 28 years of his life to traveling across the deserts of the Islamic Empire, as well as much of Europe, Southeast Asia, and China. He covered almost 75,000 miles (120,700 km) during his travels.

THE LOST CITY

Legend has it that the magnificent ancient capital, Wabar, of King 'Ad Ibn Kin'ad lay deep in the Rub'al Khali Desert, part of the Arabian Desert. The palaces were supposed to be encrusted with precious gems but the city was destroyed and has been lost for 7,000 years — covered by shifting desert sands.

ILL-FATED EXPEDITION

On January 6, 1932, Harry Philby set out with 18 men and 32 camels to discover the lost city. The Arabs call this area the "Empty Quarter" and warned him that terrible dangers lay ahead, but Philby was determined.

However, on the first night, he collapsed and turned yellow. His companions thought he was going to die from his mystery illness, but, remarkably, he came around the next morning feeling bright and breezy.

Nonetheless, the run of bad luck was set to continue. The weather turned bitterly cold and even the drinking water froze in its containers. A few days later, it became unbearably hot and they were struck by debilitating sandstorms.

EXTREME SURVIVAL

Next, their water ran out. The Arab guides were able to find wells buried deep under the sand but this was time-consuming and laborious work.

Finally, close to exhaustion, the expedition saw a distant ridge against the horizon. It took them hours to reach the top of the ridge but Philby was convinced it was the lost city.

Imagine his disappointment when they finally reached the top, only to discover that it was the rim of an old volcano and not Wabar, the lost city, at all.

PRESSING ON

The guides had had enough by now (who can blame them?) and they begged Philby to abandon the expedition. Philby was determined to salvage something from the trip and he ordered them to push on across a further 373 miles (600 km) of waterless desert.

The drought-stricken area nearly defeated the exhausted camels and men. Their food and water were just about gone when, on March 14, they emerged from the desert.

Philby's expedition was the first to cross the Empty Quarter — so although he never found his lost city, at least he got a world record as compensation.

Fact File
Deepest, Darkest Africa
In 1844, while exploring the
Kalahari Desert of southern
Africa, Dr. David Livingstone was
attacked and mauled by a lion. He
survived the attack but never
regained the full use of his left
arm. He spent eleven years
exploring the Kalahari — this was
20 years before the famous
meeting in Ujiji where Henry
Stanley uttered the famous words
"Dr. Livingstone, I presume?"

MODERN-DAY EXPLORER

In 1995, explorer Benedict Allen and three camels attempted to cross the remote desert landscape of the Skeleton Coast, where the Namib desert meets the Atlantic Ocean in south-western Africa. This was the first time the journey across this remote desert landscape had been permitted by any government of Namibia.

PREPARATION

Allen prepared for his expedition with the Himba people of the Namib. By immersing himself in the ways of these resilient, cattle-herding nomads, Allen began to understand a little about surviving in this hostile land.

Next, he traveled south to spend three weeks in the Kalahari Desert where he met his three reluctant traveling companions — the camels, Nelson, Jan, and Andries.

Unfortunately for Allen, Nelson believed he was the team leader and a battle of wills ensued, during which Allen sustained some nasty injuries from being thrown and bucked by the stubborn camels. Would you trust your life to a camel who was determined to hurt you? I'm not sure I would.

Grudgingly, a team spirit was forged and the expedition set off. Soon, the team confronted their first big obstacle — a stretch of the coast where the incoming tide meets colossal dunes. Here, Allen discovered that, contrary to popular belief, camels fare badly in dunes. They also have an instinctive fear of slopes, which his three camels had to overcome if they were to get through this hostile region safely.

By this time, Allen was suffering from cuts and abscesses that had developed when scratches were infected by camel grime and windblown sand. He had no backup vehicle, no luxuries, and no radio communications — it really was down to him and his camels to come through the ordeal relying solely on their own wits and resilience.

And now they were entering lion country . . .

LION BAIT

Entering bush country, Allen faced one of the greatest threats so far . . . sudden attack by lions or rhinos. He was advised that, at night, it was better to risk the snakes and sleep with his head protected by boulders or even a bush than to leave it exposed and risk a lion attack. Anxiously, he slept with his revolver loaded and was startled several times by ostriches and springboks but, thankfully, no lions.

As he battled on to the last leg of the journey, he struggled to keep control of his nervous but now faithful camels. At one point, Jan nearly died from exhaustion and it was only Allen's determination to get all his team to the end of the journey that saved the weakened camel — in fact, Allen even shared his precious personal drinking water with the beast! Could you be that selfless?

On December 4, 1995, three and a half months after they started, the team reached their destination. It was all Allen could do to keep his thirsty camels from rushing to the Nile to drink — where they would have been prime targets for the monster-sized Nile crocodiles. What a rotten end that would have been after achieving so much, right?

A hazardous journey but an amazing achievement, wouldn't you agree?

CHAPTER FIVE

Desert Survivor's Tip

Camels are hard to learn to ride. They sway
backward and forward and from side to side.
It's best to try to roll with them. If in
doubt, hold on to the pommel of
your saddle.

The Tuaregs, nomads who live in the Sahara,
steer camels with their feet and a rope but
you will probably need a bridle and reins
(and possibly a switch) to keep control.

Camels are able to walk 99 miles (160 km)
a day and carry enormous loads. When they
run, boy, can they run fast, so you'd better
hang on 'cuz it's a mighty long way down!

Fact File
A thirsty camel can drink 26
gallons (100 l) of water in just a
few minutes, and then store some
of this in its stomach for days.

DESERT
WARFARE
SURVIVAL
STORIES

CHAPTER SIX

DESERT WARFARE SURVIVAL STORIES

Most of us have to suffer from particularly bad luck to find ourselves in a survival situation in the desert. However, for the military, going into such hostile environments is not just a conscious decision, but it is an accepted part of the job.

In World War II, soldiers of the Allied forces, nicknamed the Desert Rats, and Rommel's troops distinguished themselves in the harsh and unforgiving environment of the North African deserts. Amazing stories of courage and determination abound and you should watch classic films like *Ice Cold in Alice* to get a taste of what went on for real.

However, there has been a more recent conflict in the desert that you may remember. The Gulf War from 1990–91 not only forced opposing armed forces into combat, but it also pitted soldiers against one of the harshest enemies of all — the desert environment.

DESERT STORM RESCUE

At 6:05 AM on January 21, 1991, Lieutenants Devon Jones and Larry Slade were flying on a mission 160 miles (257 km) inside Iraqi territory, only 30 miles (48 km) from Baghdad, when their U.S. Navy F-14 Tomcat aircraft was struck by an Iraqi missile. They had no choice but to bail out.

61

Back at base in Saudi Arabia, a helicopter crew made ready to rescue the downed airmen from the crash site before they were captured by the enemy. The race was on.

DIRE CONDITIONS

There was dense fog that morning, which hampered Special Operations Squadron Captain Tom Trask (pilot) and Major Mike Homan (copilot) as they prepared their rescue mission. Once over the Iraqi border, they were forced to drop their helicopter to a flight altitude of only 15 feet to avoid enemy radar. They had to fly in this perilous manner all the way to the crash site.

As they reached the crash vicinity, an enemy fighter appeared. Fortunately for the helicopter crew, who were sitting ducks, two U.S. Air Force F–15 Eagles picked up the enemy fighter on their radar and he knew better than to stick around.

Shaken, Captain Trask, Major Homan, and the crew continued with their search-and-rescue operation.

Unbeknownst to the rescue party, Lieutenant Slade had already been captured by the Iraqi forces (he was not released until March 4, 1991) but Lieutenant Jones had managed to evade them and was still at liberty. However, all he had was the flight suit he had on and he was exposed to the full heat of the glaring desert sun.

NO LUCK

By lunchtime, the helicopter still had not located the downed F-14 crew and, although they hated to do so, were forced to return to base to refuel. Meanwhile, a dehydrated and anxious Lieutenant Slade continued to wait and hope.

As soon as the helicopter was refueled, they flew back to the crash site and resumed their painstaking search. At 1:55 PM, the helicopter crew made radio contact with Lieutenant Jones on the ground. However, they weren't home and safe yet.

THE ENEMY CLOSE IN

At that point, one of the door gunners spotted an enemy truck heading toward Lieutenant Jones. Despite critically low fuel, two United States Air Force Thunderbolts, that were part of the search-and-rescue mission, returned and destroyed the vehicle.

Captain Trask landed the helicopter less than 150 yards (137 m) from the smoldering truck and a crewman, Sergeant Ben Pennington, helped an exhausted but grateful Lieutenant Jones into the helicopter.

The crew and a shattered Lieutenant Jones, who had managed to spend over eight hours in the scorching desert sun evading the enemy, returned safely to the base in Saudi Arabia.

Survivor's Tip

Bailing out of a plane is scary enough, but imagine you jump out and your parachute doesn't open. Would you know what to do (apart from praying, obviously)? If your parachute and reserve fail:

• Attract the attention of your fellow bailers (before they open their chutes) and, by pointing at your chute, make them understand that you have a malfunction.

• Once a companion has reached you, link arms.

• The two of you will now be falling toward Earth at a speed of about 130 miles per hour (209 kph) (terminal velocity). If your friend was to open his or her chute now, you would be torn apart because there's no way you can withstand the G-forces that triple or quadruple your weight when the chute opens. So . . .

• Now hook your arms behind your friend's chest-webbing or through the front of your friend's harness. Make sure you push your arms right through to the elbows and then hold on to your own parachute straps.

• When your friend opens the chute, you will both be jerked up severely — the pressure may even be enough to break or dislocate your arms, so brace yourself (it's better than hitting the deck at 130 miles per hour; 209 kph).

• Your friend will now steer the canopy for you both, hopefully choosing a good soft landing for the two of you. If it's only a small, fast canopy, then prepare yourself for a hard landing.

BEHIND ENEMY LINES

On the night of January 22, 1991, at a remote airfield in Saudi Arabia, under cover of darkness and in the utmost secrecy, eight members of the British SAS regiment boarded a helicopter that was to infiltrate deep behind enemy lines. Their mission, under the command of Sergeant Andy McNab, was to sever the underground communication link between Baghdad and northwest Iraq, and to seek and destroy mobile Scud launchers before Israel was provoked into entering the Gulf War. Their call sign was Bravo Two-Zero.

Each member of the patrol was laden with a mighty 180 pounds (82 kg) of equipment. Just imagine walking anywhere carrying that much. In fact, they patroled 32 miles (20 km) across flat desert to reach their objective and find a hiding place before first light.

By late evening of January 24, the patrol was discovered deep behind enemy lines. The Iraqis attacked with armor, and a fierce firefight ensued. The patrol was forced to escape. They decided to head for the Syrian border, 192 miles (120 km) to the northwest.

Survivor's Tip

If you've bailed out from a combat aircraft behind enemy lines, make sure you hide the parachute, otherwise this will give away your location to the enemy pursuers.

ESCAPE AND EVASION

That first night, in pitch darkness and with weather cold enough to freeze diesel fuel, they covered 53 miles (85 km) — that's more than two marathons! Yet they had not expected the exceptional and unseasonably cold nights of the desert winter and they began to suffer from hypothermia.

The patrol somehow got separated. Four men were captured. Three died. Only one, Chris Ryan, escaped — but in their wake lay 150 Iraqi dead and wounded.

Left on his own, Chris Ryan beat off another Iraqi attack and set out alone. He traveled at night, narrowly avoiding detection by the Iraqi villagers and coping with searing heat during the day and freezing temperatures at night. He eventually made it to Syria and from there, was flown home to recover. He weighed 176 pounds (80 kg) when he left Saudi Arabia at the start of the mission, and ten days later, when he reached Syria, he'd lost 36 pounds (16 kg), weighing only 140 pounds (63.5 kg)! For his part in the mission and his escape, Chris Ryan was awarded the Military Medal.

Desert Survivor's Tip

Escape and Evasion

Trying to evade capture in a sandy desert
is difficult. First, there is little or nothing
to hide behind or to camouflage you.
Second, if the weather is favorable, your
spoor (footprints) can remain for days. Hard
sand produces a clear footprint, whereas in
soft sand, the footprint is sufficiently deep
to leave a shadow.

It is harder for the tracker in dry,
rocky terrain but not impossible, so you must
take care not to leave rocks turned
over (these are obvious to a tracker because
they are darker on what was
the underside).

The distance between your footprints tells
the tracker how fast you're moving —the
longer the stride, the faster you're
traveling. And, the remains of a
campfire will tell him that you are rested.
The golden rule of evasion is: Never
leave a sign.

Desert Survivor's Tip

Since you are generally traveling at night and seeking shelter from the sun during the day, you are often hidden from search aircraft, so it's important to leave location signals at each resting place, if possible. Place large ground signs, made out of rocks or debris that can be easily seen from the sky, either in an arrow shape indicating the direction in which you're traveling or in a "V" shape — an international distress signal.

SHOT DOWN OVER THE DESERT

In 1942, Bob Nelson's plane was shot down over the desert. He managed to salvage a few items from the wreckage before it blew up. He collected a few cans of tomato juice, a water bottle, a flashlight and compass, and some Benzedrine, an amphetamine that gives you additional energy.

THE LONG TREK

Bob rested during the days and walked at night, signaling with his flashlight to try to attract attention. Each day he allowed himself one can of tomato juice and a little drop of water, but his meager supplies soon ran out.

One day, as his strength ebbed, he took all the Benzedrine at once and walked through the blazing heat of the desert day. Bob passed out and when he came to, he realized he had collapsed by some telegraph poles. In desperation, he managed to cut the wires hoping that this might bring someone out to fix them and they would find him.

Thankfully for Bob, someone had left some large empty oil drums at the bottom of the telegraph poles. After three days in the desert, Bob was close to death but he cut open these drums and licked the early morning condensation off the inside. This was just enough to keep him alive. Remarkable determination and ingenuity, wouldn't you say?

DELIVERANCE

As luck would have it, a camel train passed by. The nomads gave Bob his first proper drink for days. As he quenched his thirst, poor Bob was doubled up with stomach cramps as the liquid hit his shrunken stomach.

The nomads looked after Bob until he'd regained his strength. After some days, they gave him supplies and directions and he set off alone again. Of course, World War II still raged in the area so not only did Bob have to try to survive in the desert but he also had to try to avoid the enemy.

AN END IN SIGHT

Eighteen days after his plane crashed in the desert, Bob walked through the German lines. No one challenged him. However, he was captured in no-man's-land by a German patrol, just a mile from his own lines. He spent the rest of the war in a German POW camp. But, I think you'd agree, Bob Nelson was lucky to be alive and a remarkable survivor.

SETTING COURSE

Because desert nights are normally clear, you

can navigate using the stars. In the Northern Hemisphere, look for Polaris, also known as the Pole Star or North Star, because it remains static in the sky above the North Pole. So, if you can find Polaris, you have a good idea of which way is due north.

To find Polaris, look out for the constellation known as the Big Dipper, also called the Plow. It's made up of seven stars and the two stars at the end, farthest from the handle, point toward Polaris.

In the Southern Hemisphere, look for the Southern Cross, which points to true south. The Southern Star is found close to the dark area of the Milky Way stripe, at the end of an imaginary

line drawn between two stars of the Southern Cross.

Studying the stars is always interesting but, in a survival situation, it could just save your life.

Desert Survivor's Tip

Finding Your Way Using Your Watch

· Hold the watch horizontal.

· Point the hour hand at the sun.

· South lies halfway between the hour hand and the 12 o'clock position.

· In the Southern Hemisphere, use the same method but it is north that lies halfway between the two positions.

SAVING
LIVES

SAVING LIVES

There's a certain irony about trying to save lives in the desert. No sooner have you finished coping with the devastating effects of hot-weather ailments such as heatstroke and sunburn than it's time to turn your attention to the equally dangerous health threats from the bitterly cold desert nights. It really is a case of going from the sublime to the ridiculous.

All joking aside, both of these temperature extremes can be life-threatening and, if you and your party are to survive, you must be vigilant and take precautions. As with most medical conditions, prevention is better than cure and doing what you can to avoid the following ailments is a far better option than trying to treat their symptoms.

So the first rule of medical survival is to watch out for one another and at the first signs of illness, take remedial action. If it's too late to stop the onset of illness, then armed with the following advice, you might just be the one to save your friends' lives in the worst-case scenario. So, pay attention, and let's go.

SNAKEBITES

The fangs of a snake are usually positioned at the front of its jaws and leave distinctive puncture marks on the skin. If you're not certain whether a snake was poisonous or not, treat as though it were poisonous . . . although it may be easier to tell the casualty that it wasn't poisonous (yes, a white lie is OK in this situation) if you want to keep your patient calm!

TREATMENT

You're trying to prevent the poison from spreading through the body so keep the victim reassured and relaxed.

- Keep the bitten part of the body below the heart.
- Wash away any venom left on the skin, with soap if possible.
- Place a restricting bandage — NOT a tourniquet — above the bite, and bandage down over the bite. This prevents the toxin from spreading.
- If available, place the wound in cool water. (It's not applicable in the desert but if ice is available, use this.)
- You should treat the patient for shock and be aware that s/he may need artificial respiration.
- Never cut a snakebite or try to suck out the poison — it's an old wives' tale that doesn't work.

Note: This same treatment applies for spider bites and scorpion stings.

Fact File
If anti-venom is available, you are likely to survive a snakebite. If you're rushed to hospital within an hour or two of a strike, and provided you know what kind of snake it was so that the right anti-venom can be administered, you should survive.

Of course, anti-venom is rarely available in a survival situation, so remember to follow the safety tips on avoiding poisonous critters (see page 91) and bear in mind that only a small proportion of snakes are venomous. Feel better now?

HEAT CRAMPS

These uncomfortable cramps are an early warning sign that you're heading for heat exhaustion, so take heed. You'll probably experience the cramps in the muscles doing the most work, so arms, legs, and abdomen are common sites. They usually result from a lack of body salt produced by excessive sweating.

SYMPTOMS

Shallow breaths; dizziness; vomiting.

TREATMENT

Get into the shade and rest for a while. Drink water that has a little salt dissolved in it — you need only a small pinch in a large cupful.

Fact File
It takes about two weeks for the body to fully acclimatize itself to the temperatures of the desert. This is why troops are inserted into the arena of war well ahead of any planned battles in order to get accustomed to the heat before they engage with the enemy.

HEAT EXHAUSTION

Too much sun and high temperatures, coupled with loss of body fluids through sweating, can result in heat exhaustion.

SYMPTOMS

Pale cold skin, yet sweating; weak pulse; dizziness and perhaps cramps; delirium and possibly bouts of passing out.

TREATMENT

Same as for heat cramps.

HEATSTROKE

This is the most serious result of overexposure to the sun.

SYMPTOMS

Hot dry skin; a flushed and feverish face without sweating; high temperature; racing pulse; severe headache; vomiting; unconsciousness.

TREATMENT

Get into the shade and raise the head and shoulders slightly.

If you have plenty of water, dampen the casualty's undergarments with tepid water — since this is unlikely in the desert, you may just have to resort to fanning the patient.

Make sure there is plenty of ventilation.

When conscious, allow patient to sip water.

Once their temperature has returned to normal, put their clothes back on and keep warm.

Fact File
In extreme cases, heatstroke can result in brain damage or even death, so be vigilant.

SUNBURN

It may seem like a joke but real sunburn with blistering as opposed to a deep tan is a very real health risk. If more than two-thirds of the body are affected, it can prove fatal.

Get out of the sun and protect the body from further exposure. Cover blisters with a dressing but don't burst them.

Fact File

Desert people recommend cow manure as an effective poultice for boils and abscesses. Revolting though it sounds, it works remarkably well.

SUN-BLINDNESS

A temporary form of blindness caused by the intense glare of the sun, which is reflected off the sand and rocks.

SYMPTOMS

Sensitivity to glare; blinking and squinting; vision takes on a pinkish hue, which becomes redder; gritty eyes; loss of vision; sharp pain.

TREATMENT

If possible, get into the dark and bandage the eyes.

Apply soothing cool, wet bandages to eyes or forehead.
Allow time for the eyes to recover.

Desert Survivor's Tip

Sun-blindness is a very painful condition, which is best prevented. If possible, wear sunglasses or protective headgear. If not available, improvise eyeshades by cutting slits in cardboard or some other blindfold. Darken the area around the eyes using charcoal to reduce the glare.

DEHYDRATION

In the desert, where water is in short supply and you sweat profusely, it is easy to become dehydrated, i.e. lacking in water.

SYMPTOMS

Extreme thirst; lack of appetite; nausea; headache; dark, pungent yellow urine; labored breathing; fatigue; eventual delirium; swollen tongue; shriveled skin.

TREATMENT

Make sure you drink enough water, if at all possible.

Desert Survivor's Tip

Water makes up 75 percent of the body weight — approximately 11 gallons (50 liters) for the average man. Survival is unlikely if more than one-fifth of this is lost through dehydration. As dehydration becomes more advanced, you will become very weak and your mental capacity is impaired — so make your plans at the beginning when you can still think clearly — and then stick to them.

HYPOTHERMIA

Ironic though it seems, the intense cold of the desert night means that your body may not be able to generate heat as fast as it loses it and your temperature may drop below normal.

SYMPTOMS

Shivering and goose bumps; apathy and confusion; inability to respond to questions; lack of coordination; lethargy interspersed with bursts of frenetic activity; lapses of consciousness; slow, shallow breathing; a weak pulse.

TREATMENT

The casualty must be rewarmed gradually. Prevent further heat loss by sheltering from the wind and weather and replacing wet clothing with dry. Don't strip off completely, but replace a garment at a time.

Give the patient warm fluids and sugary foods (only if conscious).

One of the best ways to warm the patient is to strip them to their undergarments and get them into a sleeping bag with someone else who is warm and semi-naked — it may sound embarrassing but it works!

If not, apply warm rocks or warm hot-water bottles to strategic areas of the body where blood supply is near the surface and so is able to carry heat through the body, namely: stomach, small of back, armpits, back of neck, wrists, and between thighs; or wrap in a foil blanket.

Never give alcohol to someone suffering from hypothermia — this aggravates the condition.

Once the patient's temperature reaches normal, you're not out of the woods yet! Their body reserves have to be rebuilt until they can generate heat internally again. So be vigilant and keep administering hot drinks, etc.

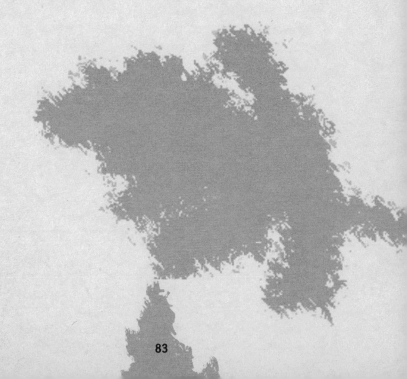

Fact File
During the Gulf War of 1991, the Bravo Two-Zero team of SAS soldiers (see page 65) traveled long distances across the desert at night. Unfortunately, the area was experiencing the worst winter weather the region had seen for years. All the soldiers suffered from hypothermia and one died of it.

So, never underestimate the danger to life and limb from the elements.

WHAT
IF . . . ?

WHAT IF . . . ?

Do you ever wonder how you might react if you found yourself in the same situation as some of the brave survivors we've just read about? Of course, some of them made mistakes but it's always easy to say "he should have done this..." or "she should never have done that ..." when you yourself are not under extreme pressure, uncomfortable, exhausted, and scared.

In fact, if one thing holds true, it's that you simply never can tell how someone will react. Some people go to pieces in a crisis while others think and act with amazing clarity, level-headedness, and purpose.

I'm sure you'd be one of the latter but here's a chance for you to come up with the solution to some interesting "What if ... ?" scenarios and to show me just how resourceful and clever your really are.

THAT SINKING FEELING

You are out walking with a group of friends on a backpacking excursion in the outback of Australia. You are well equipped with camping and cooking equipment, navigational aids, and a first aid kit in your backpack, plus a long walking stick.

You have become separated from your party and you decide to take a shortcut off the track across some open, sandy ground to try to catch up with the others.

As you get halfway across, you start to be sucked into the sand. You struggle to free yourself but your wriggling only succeeds in getting you deeper into the sand. You call desperately for your friends but no help comes. You are alone in quicksand!

It looks like you are going to have to help yourself if you are to avoid a slow and agonizing fate. How can you get out? It's your call, dude.

Desert Survivor's Solution

Pretty scary stuff, huh? In fact, it's one of my worst nightmares but, if you stay calm, you should be able to get yourself out of this predicament. Your best piece of equipment is your long walking stick — did you get that? I hope you didn't try to use any of the other equipment that I mentioned — all of which was a ruse on my part to put you off the scent of the right answer. After all, what were you planning to do with camping equipment and a first aid kit? I don't believe a Band-Aid could heal this problem.

HOW TO ESCAPE FROM QUICKSAND

1 Lay your long walking stick on the surface of the quicksand (any pole or stout stick will do, and it's worth carrying one when walking in quicksand country).

2 Lie on your back on top of the walking stick. After a short while, you should stop sinking and start to float.

3 Once you've stopped sinking, work the stick so it's at right angles to your backbone and try to get it under your hips.

4 Once your hips are over the pole, you can very slowly start to pull out one leg and then the other.

5 Get to firmer ground by the shortest route possible, but don't panic and rush or you'll sink again. Take your time.

Fact File

Quicksand is simply ordinary sand and groundwater that's welling up, mixed together so that it behaves more like a liquid. Unfortunately, unlike water, quicksand tends to cling and suck you below the surface. However, it is relatively easy to float in quicksand because of its density. So, if you don't have a stout pole with you, spread your arms and legs wide and try to float on your back to escape the deadly clutches of quicksand.

A DEADLY BITE

You're on a family trip in Monument Valley, Arizona, and are on a day's outing. You've walked all morning and are now getting hungry. While Mom and Dad unpack and lay out the picnic close to a small stream, you and your sister start to scramble up a rocky outcrop near where you've stopped. As you climb, you can see for miles and you realize that there's not another human soul as far as the eye can see.

You are nearing the top of the rocks now. You reach up to get a handhold when a searing pain shoots through your hand. You pull your hand back and realize with dread that you've been bitten. But by what? You have no idea what type of snake has bitten you, if indeed it was a snake, and you're not about to put your hand up there again to find out.

Fighting panic, you call out to your parents who are 40 feet (12 m) below. Your little sister is lower down the rock face than you but she's not a confident climber.

This is a real problem and you don't have long to think or act before the poison takes effect. What do you do next?

Desert Survivor's Solution

Did you go faint at the mere thought of finding yourself in such a situation, or have you come up with a clever plan to save yourself? Well, I hope whatever it was it didn't include getting your long-suffering parents to suck out the poison. As you'll remember from the last chapter, sucking out the poison would probably result in your poor old mom collapsing, too, and it's unlikely to save your bacon either.

I'm sure you had a stunning plan up your sleeve but, for what it's worth, my suggestion is that you send little sis down to warn your parents and get help — she may be slow but she'll be a lot quicker than you climbing with just one arm. Once safely down to ground, your parents should clean any venom off the skin and get you to dangle your arm in the cool stream. Then they should bandage down over the bite from the elbow and keep you calm and reassured.

Of course, being more knowledgeable on desert survival skills than your parents, I hope you told them right at the start to use the cell phone to call for medical assistance. The air-ambulance should be with you faster than you can shake a stick. So hang in there and I'm sure you'll get through this ordeal.

CHAPTER EIGHT

In the future, try to avoid an attack by:

～ Keeping away from a snake at all costs — never prod or poke it to get it to move.

～ No matter how hungry you are, don't try to kill a snake, it's just not worth the risk.

～ If you come across a snake in the open, back away slowly and make sure it has an escape route.

～ Always wear stout, thick leather boots and long pants when hiking in an area with poisonous snakes.

～ Be careful when you pick up rocks or logs — kick them over with your boot first or use a stick.

～ Look closely before you part bushes, pick fruit, etc., since some snakes live in trees (arboreal).

～ Shake out discarded clothing, bedding, and boots before use because cold-blooded creatures such as snakes and scorpions seek warmth — and your gear could be the closest thing to reptile heaven.

～ Be especially careful when rock climbing in snake country.

Fact File
There are about 8,000 venomous snakebites a year in the United States, of which only nine to fifteen prove fatal.

Desert Survivor's Tip
A snake coils before it strikes. To judge how far it can strike, gauge how long it is before it coils — a snake strikes at a distance of approximately half its length; it leaves half its body coiled on the ground for stability. Mind you, I wouldn't take a chance on standing just outside its range thinking I was safe, if I were you.

AUTOMOBILE TROUBLES

You're driving across the desert in a jeep with a couple of classmates and your teacher is at the wheel. It's getting late and you still have 40 miles or so to go before you get to a town. Unfortunately, your teacher swerves to miss a pothole in the road and your vehicle becomes bogged down in the soft, loose sand of the shoulder. Your teacher is rather inexperienced and, in his panic, he spins the rear wheels until one is stuck deep in the sand. At present, you're going nowhere fast — any idea on how to get you and your party to safety before night falls?

DESERT MOTORING

I expect you thought of getting all your classmates together and trying to push the jeep out as a first step. This was good thinking, but it looks like your wheel is bogged down too deeply for this to be successful.

When driving in the desert, you should always carry a spade to dig your vehicle out in just such a situation as this, and some sand mats or mesh fencing, plus pieces of wood to support the car jack in the sand. If you don't have any of this equipment — and going on your teacher's track record so far, I suspect you haven't — you can improvise.

Use the hubcaps to dig the sand out around the tire and use the floor mats to give support and traction when you gently drive out. Lowering the tire pressure will also assist. Hubcaps are very versatile, by the way, because they can also be used as a jack support in the sand if you ever need to change a wheel.

Hope you came up with something similar to get you all to safety.

Desert Survivor's Tip

The following motoring tips are useful if you need to cross the desert or outback by road at any time:

- Leave details of your plans when journeying through remote and dangerous country with someone you can trust to take action if you haven't made contact at prearranged times. Local police are usually very helpful about this.

- Never travel alone, if at all possible.

- Make sure your car is roadworthy and serviced before making the trip.

- Carry adequate supplies of water (4.25 quarts; 4 l per person per day), some food, a shovel, and mesh fencing, in case the car gets stuck in sand, and pieces of wood to go under a jack.

- If you use sand mats (or fencing) to get a bogged car out, attach them to the back of your vehicle so they're dragged behind as you pull off. This way, you don't have a long walk back to get them.

- When driving on sand, keep the vehicle in a straight line. If you have to make a turn, do it by twisting the wheel quickly around in the direction you want to go and then quickly back to the original position.

• On dirt roads, do not try to avoid every pothole, just drive carefully at a constantly safe speed.

• To make a creek crossing, check the underlying surface to make sure there is no danger of getting bogged, and check the depth and flow of water. When crossing, drive slowly in the center and keep the wheels straight in case of mud or sand.

• Watch out when overtaking large tractor-trailers, which generate dangerous dust clouds that make it impossible to see. If possible, resist the temptation to overtake.

Desert Survivor's Tip

Your vehicle can provide a great supply of survival equipment:

〜 A headlight or driving spotlight can be dismantled and reconnected to the battery to make a good signaling device.

〜 Tires can be burned during the day to give a thick cloud of black signal smoke.

〜 Oil from the sump, soaked in a rag or burned in a hubcap can provide a signal fire at night.

∿ The hood and trunk lids, together with interior seating and paneling, can provide protection against the sun and heat.

∿ Rearview mirrors can be used as excellent signaling devices, as can headlight reflectors.

∿ With patience, headlight lenses can, in some cases, be used to focus a very fine beam of sunlight to start a fire without matches.

∿ Wires connected from the battery terminals to a lightly dampened gas rag or tinder will do likewise.

∿ Hubcaps make substitute shovels.

∿ Chassis grease makes effective sunblock.

∿ Black grease smeared under the eyes reduces glare substantially.

∿ Provided there are no alcohol or detergent additives, water from the windshield washer reservoir may be used for drinking. Never drink water from the radiator, however, as it contains chemical additives.

DESERT
BRAIN-
TEASERS

DESERT BRAIN-TEASERS

If you think about it, the only way that survival skills and techniques come to light is if some poor soul goes through a grueling survival ordeal and lives to tell the tale. Of course, outdoor specialists also gather information from indigenous peoples who have generations of accumulated knowledge.

Then this hard-won information is passed on to military forces, emergency medical organizations, and search-and-rescue teams where the skills are rehearsed ready for the real thing. Training exercises like the one below are used on such courses to test a candidate's knowledge and understanding of the desert environment and his or her resourcefulness.

The situation described here is based on more than 2,000 actual cases in which men and women lived or died depending upon the survival decisions they made. Your own "life" or "death" will depend upon how well you can figure out what's of use and what is surplus to your requirements.

If you do this exercise with a few of your buddies, then it's a good test to see how well you can share your knowledge of a relatively unfamiliar situation so that you can make decisions leading to your survival (hopefully).

Let's see if you're the wily coyote of the desert I think you are, shall we.

CHAPTER NINE

DISASTER IN THE DESERT

It is mid-morning in June and you have just crash-landed in the Mojave Desert. Your light twin-engine plane, containing the body of the pilot, has completely burned out. Only the frame remains. No one else has been injured.

The pilot was able to send a Mayday signal just before you crashed. However, ground sightings taken shortly before the crash suggested that you are about 25 miles (40 km) off course from your originally filed flight plan.

A few moments before the crash the pilot told you that there was a small mining camp 70 miles (112 km) away in a southwesterly direction. The immediate area is rocky and rather barren except for the occasional cactus. The last weather report indicated that the temperature would reach 110°F (43°C), which means that the temperature within a foot of the surface will hit 130°F (54°C).

You are dressed in lightweight clothing — short-sleeved shirts, shorts, socks, and leather shoes. Everyone has a handkerchief. Collectively your pockets contain $5.73 in change, $82.00 in bills, and a ballpoint pen.

SO WHAT ARE YOU GOING TO DO?

Before the plane caught fire, your group was able to salvage the fourteen items listed on the next page. Your first task is to make a ranking of the order of importance of these items for your survival, starting with 1 for the most important, down to 14 for the least important.

You and your small group of survivors have decided to stick together (that's you and your friends for our purposes, OK) so once you have come up with your own rating, why don't you discuss your individual answers together and agree on a final group ranking. (If you'd rather just do this on your own, that's fine!)

Next, decide whether you would stay at the crash site and wait for help, or walk out.

RANKINGS

Put the order of importance for each item in the box next to it, both individually and as a group. You might want to write the table out again so that the others can't see your answers.

ITEMS

	Individual Ranking	Group Ranking
Flashlight		
Jackknife		
Sectional air map of crash site		
Plastic raincoat (large-sized)		
Magnetic compass		
Bandage kit with gauze		
.45-caliber pistol (loaded)		
Parachute (red and white)		
Bottle of salt tablets		
1 quart (.9 l) of water per person		
Book entitled *Edible Animals of the Desert*		
1 pair of sunglasses per person		
Cosmetic mirror		
1 topcoat per person		

SOLUTION

So, are you feeling confident? Think you're on your way to safety? Well, let's see, shall we. Here are the experts' ranking and rationale in order of merit:

1 THE COSMETIC MIRROR

The mirror is far and away the most important item on the list. It is the most powerful tool you have for communicating your presence to would-be rescuers. In the sunlight a simple mirror can generate between 5 and 7 million candlepower of light. That's massively bright. The reflected sunlight can even be seen beyond the horizon.

2 ONE TOPCOAT PER PERSON

Once you have a communication system to tell people where you are, the next problem is to slow down dehydration. Forty percent of the body moisture that is lost through dehydration is lost through respiration (breathing) and perspiration (sweating). You can significantly reduce moisture loss through respiration by remaining calm and inactive. Moisture loss through perspiration can be minimized by preventing hot, dry air from circulating over the skin. The coats, ironic as it may seem, are the best available means for doing this. Without them, survival time would be cut by at least one day. Surprising, isn't it.

3 ONE QUART OF WATER PER PERSON

You could probably survive about three days with just the first two items. Although a quart (.9 l) of water doesn't significantly extend your survival time, it does help to stave off the effects of dehydration. Drink the water as you become thirsty, so that you can remain as clearheaded as possible during the first day when important decisions have to be made and a shelter erected. Once dehydration begins it would be impossible to reverse it with the amount of water available in this situation. Therefore, rationing it would do no good at all. (I bet that surprised you — did you have water at the top of your list? I can see your logic if you did, so bad luck, but what about making a still?)

4 FLASHLIGHT (FOUR BATTERIES)

The only quick, reliable night-signaling device is the flashlight. With this and the mirror you have a 24-hour signaling capacity. It is also a multiple-use item during the day. The reflector and lens can be used as an additional signaling device or for starting a fire.

The battery container could be used for digging or as a water container in the distillation process (see plastic raincoat).

5 PARACHUTE (RED AND WHITE)

A parachute can serve as both a shelter and a signaling device. Use a tall cactus, such as the saguaro, as a tent pole and the parachute shrouds as tent ropes. Double- or triple-folding the parachute gives you shade dark enough to reduce the temperature underneath it by as much as 20 percent, can you believe?

6 JACKKNIFE

Although not as crucial as the first five items, the jackknife would be useful for rigging the shelter and for cutting up the very tough barrel cactus to get moisture. Its innumerable other uses earn it its high ranking.

7 PLASTIC RAINCOAT (LARGE-SIZED)

The plastic, nonporous material of the raincoat is ideal for building a solar still (see page 27). Up to a quart (.9 l) of water a day can be obtained in this way. Although this would be undoubtedly helpful, it is not enough to make any significant difference. The physical activity required to extract the water is likely to use up about twice as much body water as could be gained.

8 .45-CALIBER PISTOL (LOADED)

By the end of the second day, speech would be seriously impaired and you might be unable to walk (6–10 percent dehydration). The pistol would then be useful as a sound signaling device and the bullets as a quick fire-starter. The international distress signal is three shots in rapid succession. There have been numerous cases of survivors going undetected because they could not make any loud sounds. The butt of the pistol may also be used as a hammer.

9 A PAIR OF SUNGLASSES PER PERSON

In the intense sunlight of the desert, damage to the eyes could be a serious problem by the end of the second day. However, the dark shade of the parachute shelter would reduce the problem, as would darkening the area around the eyes with soot from the wreckage. Did you remember that tip? Using a handkerchief or compressing material as a veil with eye slits cut into it would eliminate the vision problem, but I agree, sunglasses might make things a little more comfortable and you wouldn't look like such a fool if that matters to you.

10 BANDAGE KIT WITH GAUZE

Because of the low humidity in the desert, it is one of the least infectious places in the world. Due to the fact that blood thickens with dehydration, there is little danger from bleeding unless a vein is severed. The bandages might also be used as rope, wrapping for your legs, ankles, head, and face, or as further protection against dehydration and sunlight.

11 MAGNETIC COMPASS

Apart from the possibility of using its reflective surface as an auxiliary signaling device, the compass is of little use. It could even be dangerous to have around once the effects of dehydration take hold. It might give someone the notion of walking out (is that a big enough clue to the answer to the walking-out/staying-put dilemma?).

12 SECTIONAL MAP OF THE CRASH AREA

The map might be helpful for starting a fire, for toilet paper, or one person may use it for head cover or eye shade. It might even have entertainment value. But it is essentially useless and perhaps dangerous because it, too, might encourage walking out (there we go again, dropping hints).

13 BOOK ENTITLED EDIBLE ANIMALS OF THE DESERT

The problem confronting the group is dehydration, not starvation. Any energy expended in hunting would be costly in terms of water loss. Desert animals, while plentiful, are seldom seen. They survive by lying low, as should the crash survivors. If the hunt were successful, the intake of protein would cause an increase in the amount of water used to process the protein in the body.

14 BOTTLE OF SALT TABLETS

Widespread myths about salt tablets exist. The first problem is that with dehydration and loss of water, blood salinity increases. Without lots of extra water, the salt tablets would require body water to get rid of the increased salinity. The effect would be like drinking seawater. Not a good idea.

CHECK OUT THE EXPERTS

Although the details of these training exercises vary from course to course, the basis and reasoning for this particular exercise was originated by Alonzo W. Pond, M.A. He is the former Chief of the Desert Branch of the Arctic, Desert, & Tropic Information Center of the Air Force University at Maxwell Air Force Base. During the second World War, Mr. Pond spent most of his time working with the Allied Forces in the Sahara on desert survival problems.

SCORING

So, how did you do? There were a few surprises in those answers, weren't there? Well, let's do the scoring anyway and see if you're a card-carrying desert survivor or not.

Add up the points for your top ten answers. Oh, and by the way, add 25 points to your total if you chose staying put as the right answer — after all, you hadn't strayed far from your flight path and you had sent a Mayday message, hadn't you?

Mirror — 12 points

Topcoats — 11 points

Water — 10 points

Flashlight — 9 points

Parachute — 8 points

Knife — 7 points

Raincoat — 6 points

Pistol — 5 points

Sunglasses — 4 points

Bandage kit — 3 points

Compass — 2 points

Map — 2 points

Book — 2 points

Salts — 2 points

SCORES

76–100: The applause is deafening. You did a great job. You were rescued in next to no time and are the toast of the school for keeping such a cool head in adversity.

51–75: Not bad at all. You're probably found by the rescue plane feeling a bit the worse for wear. A good first attempt.

26–50: You are severely dehydrated by now and out of your mind with delirium. You'll need some time in the hospital but you should survive your ordeal — just.

0–25: Sometimes you have to be cruel to be kind, so I won't mince my words. It's back to the drawing board for you, I'm afraid, because the buzzards are picking over your bones as we speak.

Did you fare better as an individual or as a team effort? Interesting isn't it?

CREEPY-CRAWLIES

Whether you're patting each other on the back or commiserating with each other, here's a final desert brainteaser to tax your weary gray matter:

While you are waiting to be rescued from the aircraft crash mentioned before, a motley collection of desert spiders and beetles has fallen into an empty water container. Your friend, who is nearer the container, won't tell you how many of each creature there is, but he says that their legs add up to 54. Can you work it out from his clue?

ANSWER
Spiders have 8 legs and beetles possess 6. So there can only be three spiders (3 x 8) and five beetles (5 x 6): 24 + 30 = 54.
Ta-da! It's simple when you have the answer, isn't it? Anyway, you'd have plenty of time to mull it over while waiting to be rescued in the desert if you didn't get it quite right the first time.

YOUR
DESERT
SURVIVAL
RATING

YOUR DESERT SURVIVAL RATING

Can you believe how far we've come together? It seems like no time at all since we were just starting out and you were a raw desert survival recruit. Well, you'll be surprised at just how much invaluable information you've picked up over the past few chapters, and now is your chance to show just what you've learned.

This little questionnaire will test your mettle but, just in case you've forgotten a thing or two, you'll find the answers in previous chapters of the book. So don't panic (that's not what a survivor does!), just flip back through the pages if you get stuck . . .

So, grab a pencil, put your thinking caps on, and let's get started, shall we?

1. In the desert, to avoid danger, you should always check your boots in the morning because they could be housing:

A sand
B scorpions
C stones
D dirty socks

2. Film from your camera can be improvised to make good:

A photographs
B napkins
C footwear
D sun-goggles

CHAPTER TEN

3. Your vehicle has crashed on the road crossing the desert. Although you have the equipment to dig it out, your skin is burning up in the fierce sun. What could you salvage from the car to put on your skin?

A chassis grease
B engine oil
C radiator fluid
D windshield washer fluid

4. In a hot desert climate, how much water do you need per day before you'd even think about attempting to walk out?

A 1–2 pints (.5–.95 l)
B 3–4 pints (1.4–1.9 l)
C 5–6 pints (2.4–2.8 l)
D 7–8 pints (3.3–3.8 l)

5. Nomadic desert peoples use cow manure to cure what ailment?

A warts and lesions
B a sore throat
C boils and abscesses
D scorpion stings

6. The name for the precision signaling instrument that reflects the rays of the sun with pinpoint accuracy is a

A heliotrope

B heliograph

C heliochrome

D heliometer

7. Water makes up what percentage of the human body? Is it:

A 25 percent

B 50 percent

C 75 percent

D 100 percent

8. One of these four cacti is poisonous, while you can get precious water from the other three. The flesh of which one should be avoided at all costs?

A saguaro cactus

B prickly pear cactus

C barrel cactus

D jumping cactus

9. A sangar is a type of what?
A cactus
B desert well
C garage for light aircraft
D stone shelter

10. "Desert Rat" is the name given to:
A an allied soldier fighting in North Africa in World War II
B someone who drinks other people's personal water supply
C a pallid gerbil
D a character from a James Cagney movie

11. In desert temperatures of 122°F (50°C), without any water, you would last at best:
A 2 days
B 5 days
C 7 days
D a month

12. Polaris is the name of the star that indicates the compass direction of:
A north
B south
C east
D west

ANSWERS

Did you find that a breeze or were you faltering in the doldrums? Hopefully, you sailed through it, but let's find out for sure, shall we?

1b Scorpions love the warmth of a nice, cozy boot — perhaps they have no sense of smell! You will undoubtedly find sand and stones in your boots from time to time but they certainly aren't a danger. As for smelly socks . . . I wouldn't be surprised if they're a health risk but no points for that.

2d You can get a splendid pair of goggles from the film in your camera but I don't think it would make very good footwear — and you don't need a napkin in the desert 'cuz we don't stand on ceremony! Don't interfere with it if you want to take good photos.

3a It may not look pretty, but thick chassis grease makes a pretty effective sunblock. Engine oil on the other hand will just fry the skin while radiator fluid and windshield washer fluid may be temporarily cooling but they won't prevent your skin from burning and they may contain unpleasant additives.

4d You would have to have about 7–8 pints (3.3–3.7 l) of water a day before you should even contemplate walking out — and that's a lot, I'm sure you'll agree.

5c Boils and abscesses respond remarkably well to a cow manure poultice. If you like gargling it for a sore throat you're a braver man than I. And I'm sure there are better cures for warts or scorpion stings.

6b A heliograph is an excellent signaling device whereas you may have a few problems being seen with a heliotrope (which is a small plant), a heliochrome (which is a colored photograph), or a heliometer (which measures the distance between stars)!

7c Yes, the human body is made up of a staggering 75 percent water. If you answered 100 percent, I don't want to know, right?

8a The saguaro cactus comprises up to 80 percent water but, frustratingly, its water content is not drinkable because it is poisonous to man.

9d A sangar is a stone-built shelter that could save your life in an emergency in the desert.

10a The celebrated "Desert Rats" fought bravely in the deserts of North Africa in World War II. Mind you, you could be forgiven for thinking that you might call the coward who drank your water a rat (if not worse) as well. By the way, James Cagney is associated with the phrase "you dirty rat" though he never uttered those immortal words in a movie.

11b Five days tops, I'm afraid. It's not long, is it?

12a Polaris is another name for the North Star or the Pole Star, and you were quite right, it does stay put over the North Pole and indicate due north.

So that's it then. How did you do? Top marks, I'm sure (or pretty close to it, anyway)? And if not, don't worry, you can always reread the book at your leisure — I find there's usually some interesting tip that you miss first time around. Even after all my years in the field, I don't like admitting that I still reread my survival manuals and I'm still learning.

And that's the whole point about survival techniques and extreme lifestyle skills — you can never know too much. Yet, for now, what we've shared together in this book will stand you in good stead if you ever find yourself alone and stranded in a desert environment, unlikely though that may be.

CHAPTER TEN

There is just one last thing that you should bear in mind before we part company. The people whose dramatic survival stories we've read about in this book did not deliberately put themselves in a life-or-death situation. If they'd had a choice, they would not have been forced to survive in the desert. And you must never court disaster, either. Always be suitably prepared if you have to venture into desert environments and never underestimate the dangers that these harsh and isolated locations can present.

So, until the next time we meet, I hope you've enjoyed the book and that you'll continue to thirst for more survival know-how, just as I do.